Copyright © 2021 by Adeleye Habeeb, Bsc.

Contents

BASIS OF ACCOUNTING

The basis of accounting refers to the methodology under which revenues and expenses are recognized in the financial statements of a business. When an organization refers to the basis of accounting that it uses, two primary methodologies are most likely to be mentioned:

Cash basis of Accounting.

Under this basis of accounting, a business recognizes revenue when cash is received, and expenses when bills are paid. This is the easiest approach to recording transactions, and is widely used by smaller businesses.

Accrual basis of Accounting.

Under this basis of accounting, a business recognizes revenue when earned and expenses when expenditures are consumed. This approach re□uires a greater knowledge of accounting, since accruals must be recorded at regular intervals. If a business wants to have its financial statements audited, it must use the accrual basis of accounting, since auditors will not pass judgment on financial statements prepared using any other basis of accounting.

A variation on these two approaches is the modified cash basis of accounting. This concept is most similar to the cash basis, except that longer-term assets are also recorded with accruals, so that fixed assets and loans will appear on the balance sheet. This concept better represents the financial condition of a business than does the cash basis of accounting.

The basis of accounting being used is typically listed as a disclosure in the footnotes that a business releases to outside parties as part of its financial statements. A change in the basis of accounting can be a major disclosure that would be of considerable interest to the users of financial statements, since this can have an immediate

impact on the financial results and financial
position of a business.

DOUBLE ENTRY SYSTEM

Double Entry system seeks to record every
transaction in money or money's worth in its
double aspect – the receipt of a benefit by
one account and the surrender of alike
benefit by another account, the former entry
being to the debit of the account receiving
the later to the credit of the account
surrendering.

What is Double-Entry System?

The most scientific and reliable method of accounting is the Double Entry System. One must have a clear conception of the nature of the transaction to understand the double-entry system.

Every transaction involves two parties or accounts – one account gives the benefit and the other receives it.

It is called a dual entity of transaction.

In every transaction, the account receiving a benefit is debited and the account giving benefit is credited.

The process of keeping account accepting this dual entity i.e. debiting one account for a definite amount of money and crediting the other account for the same amount is called a double-entry system.

Every transaction affects the accounting e□uation of a business. Dual change may take place between two assets.

For example, Machinery purchased on cash.

Here machinery account receives the benefit and the cash account gives the benefit or the amount of decrease in cash will give an increase of machinery for the same amount.

Again this change may take place between two liabilities.

For example; to meet up the claim of a creditor taking a long-term loan.

Here long-term liability is credited abolishing the short term liability of creditor. Besides, this change may take place between assets and liabilities.

For example; furniture purchased on credit.

Here asset is debited for a particular amount and at the same time, an e☐ual amount of liability is also credited.

Since every transaction brings changes in assets for an equal sum of money or asset and liability or liabilities, the transactions are to be recorded according to a double-entry system to know the accurate, position of assets and liabilities of a business concern.

If accounts are maintained under a double-entry system two accounts are affected.

One is debited and another is credited. This is the main principle of the double-entry system.

To make the matter clear some examples are given below;

Mr. Angel invested cash $20,000 in his business as capital. This transaction involves two accounts – Cash Account and Capital Account – Angel. For this transaction asset-cash increases for $20,000 on one side and on the other side liability increases for $20,000 as capital which is the claim of the owner.

This transaction is to be recorded debiting cash and crediting capital accounts. If the transactions are not recorded in two accounts proper results are not reflected.

Furniture purchased for $2,000. This transaction involves two accounts – a furniture account and a cash account.

For this transaction cash decreases for $2,000 and furniture increases by $2,000. Here, the furniture account is debited and the cash account is credited for $2,000 cash.

In another way, the transaction changes only. An element of accounting e□uation i.e., $A = L + P$.

It is clear from the above discussion that every transaction is to be recorded in two accounts – one is debited and the other is credited.

The main principle of double-entry system is that for every debit there is a corresponding credit for an e□ual amount of money and for every credit there is a corresponding debit for an e□ual amount of money; i.e. for every transaction one account is debited for the amount of transaction and the other account is credited for the equal amount of money.

Therefore, it can be said that the system under which every transaction is accounted in two accounts for the e□ual amount of money debiting one and crediting the other ignoring no account is called a double-entry system.

Every debit must have a corresponding credit and Vice – Versa. Double-entry Book-Keeping is a system by which every debit entry is balanced by an e□ual credit entry.

Characteristics or Fundamental Principles of Double Entry System

The double-entry system is a scientific, self-sufficient and reliable system of accounting. Following some widely accepted characteristics or principles account is kept under this system.

As a result in one side arithmetical accuracy of the transaction is ensured and on the other side ascertainment of the financial position of the business is easily possible.

Characteristics of double-entry system are stated below;

Two parties: Every transaction involves two parties – debit and credit. According to the main principles of this system, every debit of some amount creates corresponding credit or every credit creates the corresponding debit for the same amount.

Giver and receiver: Every transaction must have one giver and one receiver.

Exchange of equal amount: The amount of money of a transaction the party gives is e□ual to the amount the party receives.

Separate entity: Under this system business is treated as a separate entity from the owner. Here the business is considered as a separate entity.

Dual aspects: Every transaction is divided into two aspects. The left side of the transaction debit and the right side is credit.

Results: Under double entry system totality of debit is e□ual to the totality of credit.

Complete accounting system: Double entry system is a scientific and complete accounting system.

Through this system, the account is kept completely and no party is ignored. In fine it can be said that every transaction must possess these characteristics?

If there is an exception to this complete information will not be available in the books of accounting. As a result, the main objective of accounting will be frustrated.

The process of keeping accounts under the double-entry system;

Journal: At first transactions are recorded in the primary book of accounting called journal.

Ledger: In the second phase transactions are classified and recorded permanently in the ledger in brief.

Trial balance: In the third phase the arithmetical accuracy of the account is verified through the preparation of trial balance.

Financial statements: In the fourth or final stage through financial statements the results of all the financial activities of a year are determined.

Advantages of Double Entry System

The double-entry system is the most scientific method of keeping accounts. In the modem age, this system is accepted as the best one.

In every organization whether big or small accounts are kept under the double-entry system.

The advantages of the double-entry system are stated in brief;

Complete accounts of transactions

The double-entry system can keep complete accounts of transactions as it is based on dual aspects of each transaction; i.e. debit and credit are recorded simultaneously.

For this reason, this system maintains accounts of all parties' relating to transactions.

Verification of arithmetical accuracy

Arithmetical accuracy of accounting can be verified through the preparation of trial balance if the accounts are maintained under the double-entry system.

Under this system, every debit for a certain amount of money will have corresponding credit for an e□ual amount.

For this reason, the total amount of debt will be e□ual to the total amount of credit. It can be detected through trial balance whether two sides of accounts are equal or not and thereby the arithmetical accuracy of the account is verified.

Determining profit or loss

Under the double-entry system, profit or loss of the company for a particular accounting period can be known by preparing an income statement.

Since all accounts relating to income and expenditure are maintained properly in the ledger under the double-entry system, it becomes convenient to draw income statement at the end of a particular accounting period.

Determining the financial position

Under the double-entry system, the total assets and liabilities of a business concern are recorded properly.

As a result at the closing day of the accounting period balance sheet is prepared with the help of all assets and liabilities. Through this balance sheet financial position of the business concerned can be ascertained.

Knowing assets and liabilities

The total amount of assets and liabilities can be ascertained if the account is kept under a double-entry system and it becomes easier to settle liability and assets.

Fixation of the price of commodities

It becomes easier to fix-up the price of
commodities as the accounts are maintained
systematically under the double-entry
system.

Submission of income and VAT statements

The double-entry system being the reliable
system of keeping accounts the submission
of reliable income and VAT statement under
it are possible on the basis of which income
tax and VAT are fixed and paid.

Comparative analysis

Under this system of accounting future
course of action can be formulated by
comparing income -expenditure, asset and

liability of the current year with that of the previous year.

Increase in profit

Under this system of accounting, the picture of all incomes or profits is reflected.

It can be identified which item is more profitable for a business comparing the items relating to a profit of the current year with that of the previous year.

In this way, attempts can be made in order to make more profit.

Expenditure control

Through comparative analysis, expenditure may be controlled by curtailing expensive expenditure.

Detection and prevention of forgery

Under this system of accounts errors or forgery of accounts can easily be detected. As a result moral qualities of an accountant and other employees are upheld.

Supply of information

This system helps run the business properly supplying necessary information and statistics to the management.

Future reference

Under this system as every transaction is permanently recorded properly and completely, any necessary information can be detected easily in the future.

Easy application

It is easier to record the transactions properly in the books of accounts following the scientific method of the double-entry system.

Generally accepted method

The double-entry system being a scientific method is a generally accepted system. The accounts under double entry system become reliable and acceptable to all concerned like income tax authority, creditors etc.

Efficiency evaluation of business concern

Capacity for earning a profit and repaying liabilities can be evaluated with the help of various ratios relating to accounts from financial statements.

For example, creditors or loan givers evaluate the loan repaying capacity of a business concern with the help of the current ratio. If the ratio is 2:1 then it is assumed that the loan repaying capacity of the business concern is sound enough.

Timely step for correcting accounting errors

Accounting errors can properly be detected and taking necessary measures for correction is possible under a double-entry system of accounting; i.e. before going to the next stage the errors of accounting can be corrected.

Utility

The utility and application of this system in the accounts of all business concerns whether big, medium or small are accepted by all.

Disadvantages or Limitations of Double Entry System

The double entry system is a generally accepted scientific method. In spite of its many important advantages some limitations of it exist which are stated below:

Increased size of books of accounts

Under the double-entry system, every transaction is recorded on two sides of two accounts and in two steps (Journal & ledger) of books of accounts.

Complexity in the accounting process

Complexity arises in following rules, principles, techniques, and methods, etc. for keeping accounts under the double-entry system.

Expensive, time and labour consuming

Since the accounting process under the double-entry system is extensive, a good number of books are to be kept and a large number of employees are employed for accounting work.

As a result, it requires enough labor, time and money. Therefore, it becomes impossible to follow this system by small business concerns.

Persons of specialized knowledge re□uired

The accountant should possess both theoretical and practical knowledge of accounting for the proper keeping of accounts under the double-entry system.

An inexperienced person in accounting fails and faces problems in maintaining accounts under this double entry system

Possibility of mistake

As the accounting process under the double-entry system is complex and complicated, the possibility of errors and mistakes cannot be avoided completely.

The limited scope of application

In a small business organization, daily shopping, a cultural ceremony the application of a single entry system of accounting is more popular and advantageous than the double-entry system.

The problem of maintaining secrecy

A lot of people are engaged in maintaining accounts under the double-entry system since the accounting process is very wide and extensive.

As a result, a problem arises in maintaining the secrecy of the accounts or business.

Though there arise some problems in maintaining accounts under double entry systems, its advantages and acceptability are so wide and comprehensive that at present age in almost all field accounts is kept under this system.

WHAT IS BOOK KEEPING?

Bookkeeping involves the recording, on a daily basis, of a company's financial transactions. With proper bookkeeping, companies are able to track all information on its books to make key operating, investing, and financing decisions.

Bookkeepers are individuals who manage all financial data for companies. Without bookkeepers, companies would not be aware of their current financial position, as well as the transactions that occur within the company.

Accurate bookkeeping is also crucial to external users, which includes investors, financial institutions, or the government – people or organizations that need access to reliable information to make better investments or lending decisions. Simply put, the entire economy relies on accurate and reliable bookkeeping for both internal and external users.

Importance of Bookkeeping

Proper bookkeeping gives companies a reliable measure of their performance. It also provides information on general strategic decisions and a benchmark for its revenue and income goals. In short, once a business is up and running, spending extra time and money on maintaining proper records is critical.

Many small companies don't actually hire full-time accountants to work for them because of the cost. Instead, small companies generally hire a bookkeeper or outsource the job to a professional firm. One important thing to note here is that many people who intend to start a new business sometimes overlook the importance of matters such as keeping records of every penny spent.

The Accrual vs Cash Basis of Accounting

In order to properly implement bookkeeping, companies need to first choose which basis of accounting they will follow. Companies can choose between two basic accounting methods: the cash basis of accounting or the accrual basis of accounting. The difference between these types of accounting is based on when the company actually records a sale (money inflow) or purchase (money outflow) in the books.

Cash Basis Accrual Basis

Definition Record transaction only when cash is actually received or paid Record transaction when it occurs, even if cash is not received or paid

Example: You purchased 100 units of a product and will pay for it next month. No transaction recorded Transaction recorded through an accounts payable (liability) account

THE BASIC ACCOUNTING EQUATION

An accounting transaction is a business activity or event that causes a measurable change in the accounting e□uation. An exchange of cash for merchandise is a transaction. Merely placing an order for goods is not a recordable transaction because no exchange has taken place. In the coming sections, you will learn more about the different kinds of financial statements accountants generate for businesses.

In the previous section we described specific types of accounts that business activities fall into, namely:

Assets (what it owns)

Liabilities (what it owes to others)

Equity (the difference between assets and liabilities or what it owes to the owners)

These are the building blocks of the basic accounting equation.   The accounting equation is:

ASSETS = LIABILITIES + EQUITY

For Example:

A sole proprietorship business owes $12,000 and you, the owner personally invested $100,000 of your own cash into the business. The assets owned by the business will then be calculated as:

$12,000 (what it owes) + $100,000 (what
you invested) = $112,000 (what the
company has in assets)

Assets = Liabilities + E□uity

112,000 = 12,000 100,000

In a sole-proprietorship, e□uity is actually
Owner's E□uity. If the business in
□uestion is a corporation, equity will be
held by stockholders, which uses
stockholder's equity but the basic e□uation
is the same:

ASSETS = LIABILITIES + EQUITY

 For Example:

A business owes \$35,000 and stockholders (investors) have invested \$115,000 by buying stock in the company. The assets owned by the business will then be calculated as:

\$35, 000 (what it owes) + \$115,000 (what stockholders invested) = \$150,000 (what the company has in assets)

Assets = Liabilities + E□uity

150,000 = 35,000 115,000

Since each transaction affecting a business entity must be recorded in the accounting records based on a detailed account (remember, file folders and the chart of accounts from the previous section), analyzing a transaction before actually recording it is an important part of financial accounting. An error in transaction analysis could result in incorrect financial statements.

To further illustrate the analysis of transactions and their effects on the basic accounting e□uation, we will analyze the activities of Metro Courier, Inc., a fictitious corporation.

1. Owners invested cash

Metro Courier, Inc., was organized as a corporation on January 1, the company issued shares (10,000 shares at $3 each) of common stock for $30,000 cash to Ron Chaney, his wife, and their son. The $30,000 cash was deposited in the new business account.

Transaction analysis: The new corporation received $30,000 cash in exchange for ownership in common stock (10,000 shares at $3 each).

We want to increase the asset Cash and increase the equity Common Stock.

Assets Equity

Transaction Cash Common Stock

1. Owner invested cash + 30,000 + 30,000

Let's check the accounting equation:
Assets $30,000 = Liabilities $0 + Equity $30,000

2. Purchased equipment for cash

Metro paid $ 5,500 cash for e□uipment (two computers).

Transaction analysis:

The new corporation purchased new asset (e□uipment) for $5,500 and paid cash.

We want to increase the asset Equipment and decrease the asset Cash since we paid cash.

Assets E□uity

Transaction Cash E□uipment Common Stock

1. Owner invested cash + 30,000 +30,000

2. Purchased e□uipment for cash – 5,500 +5,500

Balance: 24,500 5,500 30,000

Let's check the accounting e□uation:
Assets $30,000 (Cash $24,500 + E□uipment $5,500) = Liabilities $0 + E□uity $30,000

3. Purchased truck for cash

Metro paid $ 8,500 cash for a truck.

Transaction analysis:

The new corporation purchased new asset (truck) for $8,500 and paid cash.

We want to increase the asset Truck and decrease the asset cash for $8,500.

Assets   Equity

Transaction Cash Equipment Truck Common Stock

1. Owner invested cash +30,000   +30,000

2. Purchased equipment for cash – 5,500 +5,500

3. Purchased truck for cash -8,500 + 8,500

Balance: 16,000 5,500 8,500 30,000

Let's check the accounting equation: Assets $30,000 (Cash $16,000 + Equipment $5,500 + Truck $8,500) = Liabilities $0 + Equity $30,000

4. Purchased supplies on account.

Metro purchased supplies on account from Office Lux for $500.

Transaction analysis:

The new corporation purchased new asset (supplies) for $500 but will pay for them later.

We want to increase the asset Supplies and increase what we owe with the liability Accounts Payable.

Assets =   Liabilities + E☐uity

Transaction Cash Supplies Equipment Truck Accounts Payable Common Stock

1. Owner invested cash +30,000   +30,000

2. Purchased equipment for cash -5,500 +5,500

3. Purchased truck for cash -8,500   + 8,500

4. Purchased supplies on account. + 500 +500

Balance: 16,000 500 5,500 8,500 500 30,000

Let's check the accounting equation: Assets $30,500 (Cash $16,000+ Supplies $500 + Equipment $5,500 + Truck $8,500) = Liabilities $500 + Equity $30,000

5. Making a payment to creditor.

Metro issued a check to Office Lux for $300 previously purchased supplies on account.

Transaction analysis:

The corporation paid $300 in cash and reduced what they owe to Office Lux.

We want to decrease the liability Accounts Payable and decrease the asset cash since we are not buying new supplies but paying for a previous purchase.

Assets =   Liabilities + Equity

Transaction Cash Supplies E□uipment Truck Accounts Payable Common Stock

1. Owner invested cash +30,000   +30,000

2. Purchased e□uipment for cash -5,500 +5,500

3. Purchased truck for cash -8,500   +8,500

4. Purchased supplies on account. +500 +500

5. Making a payment to creditor. -300   -300

Balance: 15,700 500 5,500 8,500 200 30,000

Let's check the accounting equation: Assets $30,200 (Cash $15,700 + Supplies $500 + E□uipment $5,500 + Truck $8,500) = Liabilities $200 + Equity $30,000

6. Making a payment in advance.

Metro issued a check to Rent Commerce, Inc. for $1,800 to pay for office rent in advance for the months of February and March.

Transaction analysis (to save space we will look at the effects of each of the remaining transactions only):

The corporation prepaid the rent for next two months making an advanced payment of $1,800 cash.

We will increase an asset account called Prepaid Rent (since we are paying in advance of using the rent) and decrease the asset cash.

Assets

Transaction Cash Prepaid Rent

Previous Balance $ 15,700

6. Making a payment in advance. -1,800 +
1,800

Balance: 13,900 1,800

The only account balances that changed
from transaction 5 are Cash and Prepaid
Rent. All other account balances remain
unchanged. The new accounting e☐uation
would be: Assets $30,200 (Cash $13,900 +
Supplies $500 + Prepaid Rent $1,800 +
E☐uipment $5,500 + Truck $8,500) =
Liabilities $200 + Equity $30,000

7. Selling services for cash.

During the month of February, Metro Corporation earned a total of $50,000 in revenue from clients who paid cash.

Transaction analysis:

The corporation received $50,000 in cash for services provided to clients.

We want to increase the asset Cash and increase the revenue account Service Revenue.

Assets Revenues

Transaction Cash Service Revenue

Previous Balance $ 13,900

7. Selling services for cash   . + 50,000 +
50,000

Balance: $ 63,900 $ 50,000

Wait a minute…the accounting e□uation is
ASSETS = LIABILITIES + EQUITY and it
does not have revenue or expenses…where
do they fit in? Revenue – Expenses equals
net income. Net Income is added to E□uity
at the end of the period. Assets $80,200
(Cash $63,900 + Supplies $500 + Prepaid
Rent $1,800 + E□uipment $5,500 + Truck
$8,500)= Liabilities $200)+ E□uity $80,000
(Common Stock $30,000 + Net Income
$50,000). Note: This does not mean
revenue and expenses are e□uity accounts!

8. Selling services on credit.

Metro Corporation earned a total of $10,000 in service revenue from clients who will pay in 30 days.

Transaction analysis:

Metro performed work and will receive the money in the future.

We record this as an increase to the asset account Accounts Receivable and an increase to service revenue.

Assets Revenues

Transaction Accounts Receivable Service Revenue

Previous Balance $ 50,000

8. Selling services on credit. + 10,000 +
10,000

Balance: $ 10,000 $ 60,000

Remember, all other account balances
remain the same. The only changes are the
addition of Accounts Receivable and an
increase in Revenue. Assets $90,200 (Cash
$63,900 + Accounts Receivable $10,000 +
Supplies $500 + Prepaid Rent $1,800 +
E□uipment $5,500 + Truck $8,500)=
Liabilities $200 + E□uity $90,000
(Common Stock $30,000 + Net Income
$60,000).

9. Collecting accounts receivable.

Metro Corporation collected a total of $5,000 on account from clients who owned money for services previously billed.

Transaction analysis:

Metro received $5,000 from customers for work we have already billed (not any new work).

We want to increase the asset Cash and decrease (what we will receive later from customers) the asset Accounts Receivable.

Assets

Transaction Cash Accounts Receivable

Previous Balance $ 63,900 $ 10,000

9. Collecting accounts receivable. + 5,000 – 5,000

Balance: $ 68,900 $ 5,000

Assets $90,200 (Cash $68,900 + Accounts Receivable $5,000 + Supplies $500 + Prepaid Rent $1,800 + Equipment $5,500 + Truck $8,500)= Liabilities $200 + E□uity $90,000 (Common Stock $30,000 + Net Income $60,000).

10. Paying office salaries.

Metro Corporation paid a total of $900 for office salaries.

Transaction analysis:

The corporation paid $900 to its employees.

We will increase the expense account
Salaries Expense and decrease the asset
account Cash.

Assets Expenses

Transaction Cash Salary Expense

Previous Balance $ 68,900

10. Paying Office Salaries. – 900 + 900

Balance: $ 68,000 $ 900

Remember, net income is calculated as
Revenue – Expenses and is added to E□uity.
The new accounting equation would show:
Assets $89,300 (Cash $68,000 + Accounts
Receivable $5,000 + Supplies $500 +
Prepaid Rent $1,800 + Equipment $5,500 +

Truck $8,500)= Liabilities $200 + E□uity
$89,100 (Common Stock $30,000 + Net
Income $59,100 from revenue of $60,000 –
expenses $900).

11. Paying utility bill.

Metro Corporation paid a total of $1,200 for
utility bill.

Transaction analysis:

The corporation paid $1,200 in cash for
utilities.

We will increase the expense account Utility Expense and decrease the asset Cash.

Assets Expense

Transaction Cash Utilities Expense

Previous Balance $ 68,000

11. Paying Utility Bill – 1,200 + 1,200

Balance: $ 66,800 $ 1,200

The final accounting equation would be: Assets $88,100 (Cash $66,800 + Accounts Receivable $5,000 + Supplies $500 + Prepaid Rent $1,800 + Equipment $5,500 + Truck $8,500) = Liabilities $200 + Equity $87, 900 (Common Stock $30,000 + Net Income $57,900 from revenue of $60,000 – salary expense $900 – utility expense $1,200).

ACCOUNTING PRINCIPLES

Accounting principles are the general rules and guidelines that companies are re□uired to follow when reporting all accounts and financial data.

Maintain and manage your business practices with Debitoor's online accounting platform to help you stay on top of your financial reporting.

Whilst there is currently no universally standardised accepted accounting principles, there are various accounting frameworks which set the standard body. The most common accounting principle frameworks used are IFRS, UK GAAP, and US GAAP. There are both similarities and differences between these three frameworks, where GAAP is more rule-based whilst IFRS is more principle based.

Why are accounting principles important?

The purpose of having - and following - accounting principles is to be able to communicate economic information in a language that is acceptable and understandable from one business to another. Companies that release their financial information to the public are required to follow these principles in preparation of their statements.

Depending on the characteristics of a company or entity, the company law and other regulations determine which accounting principles they are required to apply. The standard accounting principles are collectively known as Generally Accepted Accounting Principles (GAAP). GAAP provides the framework foundation of accounting standards, concepts, objectives and conventions for companies, serving as a guide of how to prepare and present financial statements.

Why are generally accepted accounting principles needed?

GAAP aims to regulate and standardise accountancy practices by providing a framework to ensure companies and organisations are transparent and honest in their financial reporting. Accounting principles serve as a doctrine for accountants theory and procedures, in doing their accounting systems.

Accounting principles ensure that companies follow certain standards of recording how economic events should be recognised, recorded, and presented. External stakeholders (for example investors, banks, agencies etc.) rely on these principles to trust that a company is providing accurate and relevant information in their financial statements.

Examples of accounting principles

There are some of the main accounting principles and guidelines, listed under US GAAP:

Conservatism principle - In situations where there are two acceptable solutions for reporting an item, the accountant should 'play it safe' by choose the less favourable outcome. This concept allows accountants to anticipate future losses, rather than future gains.

Consistency principle - The consistency principle states that once you decide on an accounting method or principle to use in your business, you need to stick with and follow this method throughout your accounting periods.

Cost principle - A business should record their assets, liabilities and e□uity at the original cost at which they were bought or sold. The real value may change over time (e.g. depreciation of assets/inflation) but this is not reflected for reporting purposes.

Economic entity principle - The transactions of a business should be kept and treated separately to that of its owners and other businesses.

Full disclosure principle - Any important information that may impact the reader's understanding of a business's financial statements should be disclosed or included alongside to the statement.

Going concern principle - The concept that assumes a business will continue to exist and operate in the foreseeable future, and not li□uidate. This allows a business to defer some prepaid expenses (accrued) to future accounting periods, rather than recognise them all at once.

Matching principle - The concept that each revenue recorded should be matched and recorded with all the related expenses, at the same time. Specifically in accrual accounting, the matching principle states that for every debit there should be a credit (and vice versa).

Materiality principle - An item is considered 'material' if it would affect or influence the decision of a reasonable individual reading the company's financial statements. This concept states that accountants must be sure to include and report all material items in the financial statement.

Monetary unit principle - Businesses should only record transactions that can be expressed in terms of a stable unit of currency.

Reliability principle - The reliability principle is used as a guideline in determining which financial information should be presented in the accounts of a business.

Revenue recognition principle - Companies should record their revenues when it is recognised, or in the same time period of when it was accrued (rather than when it was received).

Time period principle - A business should report their financial statements (income statement/balance sheet) appropriate to a specific time period.

Accounting principles and Debitoor

A growing business can benefit from an automated accounting system such as Debitoor invoicing software. Debitoor allows a businesses to generate and produce financial reports at any given time. Additionally, it can assist you in managing your accounts and reporting, and help determine the current financial standing of your business.

FINANCIAL ACCOUNTING

Financial accounting is the recording and reporting of a company's transactions. These transactions are presented in financial reports that provide an insight into a company's activities and financial position.

Businesses report their performance on a regular basis, and it is vital to have a thorough understanding of the financial statements in order to undertake effective analysis.

For the majority of countries, it is a requirement that companies report their financial statements on a regular basis. How they must report their financial data will vary country to country, but most will follow one of two frameworks:

US Generally Accepted Accounting Principles (US GAAP) or

International Financial Reporting Standards (IFRS)

The frameworks provide a list of rules and guidelines to help companies prepare their financial statement. The frameworks are based on four main principles:

Consistency (calculations are completed consistently period on period)

Going concern (the business will continue for the foreseeable future)

Accruals (revenues and expenses are recognized as incurred)

Offsetting (items are not netted off unless re□uired by rules)

Most businesses produce audited financial statements once a year with periodic announcements throughout. Within the US, the yearly reports are called 10Ks and the □uarterlies are 10Qs. Outside the US, the yearly reports are normally annual reports with the periodic ones being referred to as interim reports.

The primary beneficiaries of these reports include investors, creditors and lenders. It is essential the reports are prepared according to one of the two frameworks to fairly reflect the financial results and condition of the company.

Components of Financial Statements

Most businesses often comprise of many individual legal entities which are part of the "family" of business or group. The financial reports cover all members of the family and are normally referred to as consolidated.

Financial statements are generally made up of the following key parts:

Management discussion and analysis (MD&A) is produced by the management of the company, who address the performance of the business. The report outlines the reasons for the company's performance, whether this be positive or negative. Often the report is tainted with a biased view but is still very useful for providing further information to analysts. Management will include both □ualitative and □uantitative assessments of the company, as well as future plans or projects.

Next are the financial statements and these provide a record of an organization's activities and financial position. The income statement, balance sheet and cash flow statement are known as the three "key" statements. These outline the company's total income and expenses across a period, its resources and financial obligations at a specified point in time, and the company's net cash flow. A strong understanding of their content is second nature to an effective analyst.

The footnotes are the final section of the report and provide supporting calculations and additional detail to the statements. Footnotes can be formed of many pages and are a goldmine of data.

Understanding the fundamentals of these reports is essential when reviewing a company. Professionals from an array of industries will need to understand what these reports show and how to read them. The ability to read and analyze the reports is vital to build a successful career in the finance industry.

FINANCIAL STATEMENTS

There are four main financial statements. They are: (1) balance sheets; (2) income statements; (3) cash flow statements; and (4) statements of shareholders' e□uity. Balance sheets show what a company owns and what it owes at a fixed point in time. Income statements show how much money a company made and spent over a period of time. Cash flow statements show the exchange of money between a company and

the outside world also over a period of time.
The fourth financial statement, called a
"statement of shareholders' e□uity," shows
changes in the interests of the company's
shareholders over time.

Let's look at each of the first three financial
statements in details.

Balance Sheets

A balance sheet provides detailed
information about a company's assets,
liabilities and shareholders' e□uity.

Assets are things that a company owns that
have value. This typically means they can

either be sold or used by the company to make products or provide services that can be sold. Assets include physical property, such as plants, trucks, e□uipment and inventory. It also includes things that can't be touched but nevertheless exist and have value, such as trademarks and patents. And cash itself is an asset. So are investments a company makes.

Liabilities are amounts of money that a company owes to others. This can include all kinds of obligations, like money borrowed from a bank to launch a new product, rent for use of a building, money owed to suppliers for materials, payroll a company owes to its employees, environmental cleanup costs, or taxes owed to the government. Liabilities also include obligations to provide goods or services to customers in the future.

Shareholders' equity is sometimes called capital or net worth. It's the money that would be left if a company sold all of its assets and paid off all of its liabilities. This leftover money belongs to the shareholders, or the owners, of the company.

The following formula summarizes what a balance sheet shows:

ASSETS = LIABILITIES + SHAREHOLDERS' EQUITY

A company's assets have to equal, or "balance," the sum of its liabilities and shareholders' e□uity.

A company's balance sheet is set up like the basic accounting e□uation shown above. On the left side of the balance sheet, companies list their assets. On the right side, they list their liabilities and shareholders' e□uity. Sometimes balance sheets show assets at the top, followed by liabilities, with shareholders' e□uity at the bottom.

Assets are generally listed based on how
□uickly they will be converted into cash.
Current assets are things a company expects
to convert to cash within one year. A good
example is inventory. Most companies
expect to sell their inventory for cash within
one year. Noncurrent assets are things a
company does not expect to convert to cash
within one year or that would take longer
than one year to sell. Noncurrent assets
include fixed assets. Fixed assets are those
assets used to operate the business but that
are not available for sale, such as trucks,
office furniture and other property.

Liabilities are generally listed based on their
due dates. Liabilities are said to be either
current or long-term. Current liabilities are

obligations a company expects to pay off within the year. Long-term liabilities are obligations due more than one year away.

Shareholders' e□uity is the amount owners invested in the company's stock plus or minus the company's earnings or losses since inception. Sometimes companies distribute earnings, instead of retaining them. These distributions are called dividends.

A balance sheet shows a snapshot of a company's assets, liabilities and shareholders' e□uity at the end of the reporting period. It does not show the flows into and out of the accounts during the period.

Income Statements

An income statement is a report that shows how much revenue a company earned over a specific time period (usually for a year or some portion of a year). An income statement also shows the costs and expenses associated with earning that revenue. The literal "bottom line" of the statement usually shows the company's net earnings or losses. This tells you how much the company earned or lost over the period.

Income statements also report earnings per share (or "EPS"). This calculation tells you how much money shareholders would receive if the company decided to distribute all of the net earnings for the period. (Companies almost never distribute all of their earnings. Usually they reinvest them in the business.)

To understand how income statements are set up, think of them as a set of stairs. You start at the top with the total amount of sales made during the accounting period. Then you go down, one step at a time. At each step, you make a deduction for certain costs or other operating expenses associated with earning the revenue. At the bottom of the stairs, after deducting all of the expenses, you learn how much the company actually earned or lost during the accounting period. People often call this "the bottom line."

At the top of the income statement is the total amount of money brought in from sales of products or services. This top line is often referred to as gross revenues or sales. It's called "gross" because expenses have not been deducted from it yet. So the number is "gross" or unrefined.

The next line is money the company doesn't expect to collect on certain sales. This could be due, for example, to sales discounts or merchandise returns.

When you subtract the returns and allowances from the gross revenues, you arrive at the company's net revenues. It's called "net" because, if you can imagine a net, these revenues are left in the net after the deductions for returns and allowances have come out.

Moving down the stairs from the net revenue line, there are several lines that represent various kinds of operating expenses. Although these lines can be reported in various orders, the next line after net revenues typically shows the costs of the sales. This number tells you the amount of money the company spent to produce the goods or services it sold during the accounting period.

The next line subtracts the costs of sales from the net revenues to arrive at a subtotal called "gross profit" or sometimes "gross margin." It's considered "gross" because there are certain expenses that haven't been deducted from it yet.

The next section deals with operating expenses. These are expenses that go toward supporting a company's operations for a given period – for example, salaries of administrative personnel and costs of researching new products. Marketing expenses are another example. Operating expenses are different from "costs of sales," which were deducted above, because operating expenses cannot be linked directly to the production of the products or services being sold.

Depreciation is also deducted from gross profit. Depreciation takes into account the wear and tear on some assets, such as machinery, tools and furniture, which are used over the long term. Companies spread the cost of these assets over the periods they are used. This process of spreading these costs is called depreciation or amortization. The "charge" for using these assets during the period is a fraction of the original cost of the assets.

After all operating expenses are deducted from gross profit, you arrive at operating profit before interest and income tax expenses. This is often called "income from operations."

Next companies must account for interest income and interest expense. Interest income is the money companies make from keeping their cash in interest-bearing savings accounts, money market funds and the like.

On the other hand, interest expense is the money companies paid in interest for money they borrow. Some income statements show interest income and interest expense separately. Some income statements combine the two numbers. The interest income and expense are then added or subtracted from the operating profits to arrive at operating profit before income tax.

Finally, income tax is deducted and you arrive at the bottom line: net profit or net losses. (Net profit is also called net income or net earnings.) This tells you how much the company actually earned or lost during the accounting period. Did the company make a profit or did it lose money?

Earnings Per Share or EPS

Most income statements include a calculation of earnings per share or EPS. This calculation tells you how much money shareholders would receive for each share of stock they own if the company distributed all of its net income for the period.

To calculate EPS, you take the total net income and divide it by the number of outstanding shares of the company.

Cash Flow Statements

Cash flow statements report a company's inflows and outflows of cash. This is important because a company needs to have enough cash on hand to pay its expenses and purchase assets. While an income statement can tell you whether a company made a profit, a cash flow statement can tell you whether the company generated cash.

A cash flow statement shows changes over time rather than absolute dollar amounts at a point in time. It uses and reorders the information from a company's balance sheet and income statement.

The bottom line of the cash flow statement shows the net increase or decrease in cash for the period. Generally, cash flow statements are divided into three main parts. Each part reviews the cash flow from one of three types of activities: (1) operating activities; (2) investing activities; and (3) financing activities.

Operating Activities

The first part of a cash flow statement analyzes a company's cash flow from net income or losses. For most companies, this section of the cash flow statement reconciles the net income (as shown on the income statement) to the actual cash the company received from or used in its operating activities. To do this, it adjusts net income for any non-cash items (such as adding back depreciation expenses) and adjusts for any cash that was used or provided by other operating assets and liabilities.

Investing Activities

The second part of a cash flow statement shows the cash flow from all investing activities, which generally include purchases or sales of long-term assets, such as property, plant and equipment, as well as investment securities. If a company buys a piece of machinery, the cash flow statement would reflect this activity as a cash outflow from investing activities because it used cash. If the company decided to sell off some investments from an investment portfolio, the proceeds from the sales would show up as a cash inflow from investing activities because it provided cash.

Financing Activities

The third part of a cash flow statement shows the cash flow from all financing activities. Typical sources of cash flow include cash raised by selling stocks and bonds or borrowing from banks. Likewise, paying back a bank loan would show up as a use of cash flow.

Read the Footnotes

A horse called "Read The Footnotes" ran in the 2004 Kentucky Derby. He finished seventh, but if he had won, it would have been a victory for financial literacy proponents everywhere. It's so important to read the footnotes. The footnotes to financial statements are packed with information. Here are some of the highlights:

Significant accounting policies and practices – Companies are re□uired to disclose the accounting policies that are most important to the portrayal of the company's financial condition and results. These often re□uire management's most difficult, subjective or complex judgments.

Income taxes – The footnotes provide detailed information about the company's current and deferred income taxes. The information is broken down by level – federal, state, local and/or foreign, and the main items that affect the company's effective tax rate are described.

Pension plans and other retirement programs – The footnotes discuss the company's pension plans and other retirement or post-employment benefit programs. The notes contain specific information about the assets and costs of these programs, and indicate whether and by how much the plans are over- or under-funded.

Stock options – The notes also contain information about stock options granted to officers and employees, including the method of accounting for stock-based compensation and the effect of the method on reported results.

Read the MD&A

You can find a narrative explanation of a company's financial performance in a section of the □uarterly or annual report entitled, "Management's Discussion and Analysis of Financial Condition and Results of Operations." MD&A is management's opportunity to provide investors with its view of the financial performance and condition of the company. It's management's opportunity to tell investors what the financial statements show and do not show, as well as important trends and risks that have shaped the past or are reasonably likely to shape the company's future.

The SEC's rules governing MD&A re□uire disclosure about trends, events or uncertainties known to management that would have a material impact on reported financial information. The purpose of MD&A is to provide investors with information that the company's management believes to be necessary to an understanding of its financial condition, changes in financial condition and results of operations. It is intended to help investors to see the company through the eyes of management. It is also intended to provide context for the financial statements and information about the company's earnings and cash flows.

Financial Statement Ratios and Calculations

You've probably heard people banter around phrases like "P/E ratio," "current ratio" and "operating margin." But what do these terms mean and why don't they show up on financial statements? Listed below are just some of the many ratios that investors calculate from information on financial statements and then use to evaluate a company. As a general rule, desirable ratios vary by industry.

If a company has a debt-to-equity ratio of 2 to 1, it means that the company has two dollars of debt to every one dollar shareholders invest in the company. In other words, the company is taking on debt at twice the rate that its owners are investing in the company.

Inventory Turnover Ratio = Cost of Sales / Average Inventory for the Period

If a company has an inventory turnover ratio of 2 to 1, it means that the company's inventory turned over twice in the reporting period.

Operating Margin = Income from Operations / Net Revenues

Operating margin is usually expressed as a percentage. It shows, for each dollar of sales, what percentage was profit.

P/E Ratio = Price per share / Earnings per share

If a company's stock is selling at $20 per share and the company is earning $2 per share, then the company's P/E Ratio is 10 to 1. The company's stock is selling at 10 times its earnings.

Working Capital = Current Assets – Current Liabilities

Debt-to-e□uity ratio compares a company's total debt to shareholders' equity. Both of these numbers can be found on a company's balance sheet. To calculate debt-to-e□uity ratio, you divide a company's total liabilities by its shareholder e□uity, or

Inventory turnover ratio compares a company's cost of sales on its income statement with its average inventory balance for the period. To calculate the average inventory balance for the period, look at the inventory numbers listed on the balance sheet. Take the balance listed for the period of the report and add it to the balance listed for the previous comparable period, and then divide by two. (Remember that balance sheets are snapshots in time. So the inventory balance for the previous period is the beginning balance for the current period, and the inventory balance for the current period is the ending balance.) To calculate the inventory turnover ratio, you divide a company's cost of sales (just below the net revenues on the income statement) by the average inventory for the period, or

Operating margin compares a company's operating income to net revenues. Both of these numbers can be found on a company's income statement. To calculate operating margin, you divide a company's income from operations (before interest and income tax expenses) by its net revenues, or

P/E ratio compares a company's common stock price with its earnings per share. To calculate a company's P/E ratio, you divide a company's stock price by its earnings per share, or

Working capital is the money leftover if a company paid its current liabilities (that is, its debts due within one-year of the date of the balance sheet) from its current assets.

* 9 7 9 8 7 0 8 5 8 7 7 8 7 *